HOW TO BUILD MUSCLE

SANKHADWIP KAR

This book is dedicated to those superior males who wants to build an aesthetic body , to build their muscle.

Building body is not a bad thing, it will bring a confidence in new which will help you in your future.

Intially you may face problem in your exercise but if you stay consistent , you will definately make it!

Contents

Introduction

A muscle is a group of muscle tissues which contract together to produce a force. A muscle consists of fibres of muscle cells surrounded by protective tissue, bundled together many more fibres, all surrounded in a thick protective tissue. A muscle uses ATP to contract and shorten, producing a force on the objects it is connected to. There are several types of muscle, which act on various parts of the body.

Contents Of This Table

Basics of Muscle

FUNCTIONS OF MUSCLES IN OUR BODY

Whether it is the largest muscle in your body or the tiny muscle controlling the movement of your eye, every muscle functions in a similar manner. A signal is sent from the brain along a bundle of nerves. The electronic and chemical message is passed quickly from nerve cell to nerve cell and finally arrives at the motor end plate. This interface between the muscle and nerve cells releases a chemical signal, acetylcholine, which tells the muscle fiber to contract. This message is distributed to all the cells in the fiber connected to the nerve.

This signal causes the myosin proteins to grab onto the actin filaments around them. These are the purple proteins in the image below. Myosin uses ATP as an energy source to crawl along the green filament, actin. As you can see, the many small heads of the myosin fibers crawling along the actin filaments effectively shortens the length of each muscle cell. The cells, which are connected end-to-end in a long fibers, contract at the same time and shorten the whole fiber.

When a signal is sent to an entire muscle or group of muscles, the resulting contraction results in movement or force being applied.A muscle can be used in many different ways throughout the body. A certain muscle might contract rarely with a lot of force, whereas a different muscle will contract continually with minimal force. Animals have developed a plethora of uses for the forces a muscle can create. Muscles have evolved for flying, swimming, and running. They have also evolved to be pumps used in the circulatory and digestive systems. The heart is a specialized muscle, which is uses exclusively for pumping blood throughout the body. These different types of muscle will be discussed below.

CHAPTER TWO

BASIC ODF BODY TYPE

There are basically three types of body types in our human body.

- *ENDOMORPH*

- *ECTOMORPH*

- *MESOMORPH*

Endomorph: At the other end of the spectrum is the endomorph, whose body type is opposite the ectomorph. Other traits include:

Stocky, solid build

Typically shorter than average height

Thick arms and legs

Strong upper legs

Gains muscle easily

Slow metabolism

Undefined, soft muscles

Gains muscle and fat very easily

Difficulty losing fat

Endomorphs have the potential to gain muscle quickly with the appropriate bodybuilding workout. Cardio is always recommended for weight control, which is often a challenge when the metabolism is slow. This body type also needs to maintain a balanced caloric intake to avoid excess weight gain.

Knowing your body type and its typical characteristics help explain and give insight to the many unknowns and challenges men often deal with when dieting and bodybuilding. It's one more tool to use to maximize your greatest assets, while minimizing the rest. There's tons of information online regarding the various body types and methods to enhance the lives they're attached to. Take advantage of this knowledge and watch yourself morph into a better you!

Ectomorph: Known as a "Hardgainer", the ectomorph body type is the leanest of the three types. Other traits include:

Fast metabolism

Difficulty gaining weight

Lean muscle mass

Very low body fat index

Very thin, often lanky

A small frame and delicate bone structure

Narrow or small shoulders

Underdeveloped chest

Any height, but is often seen in tall men

The greatest challenge ectomorphs have is gaining weight, hence the term" hardgainer". Regardless of the reason, most have a fast metabolism that burns calories quicker than normal; making weight and muscle gain difficult. As a result, high caloric intake and customized workouts that focus on large muscle groups are needed, in order for the hardgainer to increase and maintain weight and muscle mass. Success is possible, but the process is often slow. Finding a suitable workout and diet is key.

Mesomorph: The most common male body type, mesomorphs have an advantage at the gym. Other traits include:

Athletic build

Well defined muscles

Big boned with a sturdy frame

Rectangular shaped body

Typically of average height

Gains muscle easily

Generally strong

Normal metabolism

Gains fat fairly easily

Mesomorphs, with their heavier bone and muscle structure, have an easy time of gaining muscle and maintaining an athletic physique. With a healthy metabolism that burns calories at a normal pace, the mesomorph can gain and lose weight easily. Still, attention should be given to his caloric intake, especially as he ages, since fat is no stranger to this body type. Bodybuilding routines are typical and require no special considerations like the Ectomorph's does. Cardio should always be a part of his workout program, in order to maintain weight.

CHAPTER THREE

HOW YOU CAN BUILD MUSCLES

9 tips for how to build muscles:-

Maximize muscle building

The more protein your body stores—in a process called protein synthesis—the larger your muscles grow. But your body is constantly draining its protein reserves for other uses—making hormones, for instance.The result is less protein available for muscle building. To counteract that, you need to "build and store new proteins faster than your body breaks down old proteins," says Michael Houston, Ph.D., a professor of nutrition at Virginia Tech University.

Shoot for about 1 gram of protein per pound of body weight, which is roughly the maximum amount your body can use in a day, according to a landmark study in the Journal of Applied Physiology.

For example, a 160-pound man should consume around 160 grams of protein a day—the amount he'd get from an 8-ounce chicken breast, 1 cup of cottage cheese, a roast-beef sandwich, two eggs, a glass of milk, and 2 ounces of peanuts. Split the rest of your daily calories equally between carbohydrates and fats.

Eat More

In addition to adequate protein, you need more calories. Use the following formula to calculate the number you need to take in daily to gain 1 pound a week. (Give yourself 2 weeks for results to show up on the bathroom scale. If you haven't gained by then, increase your calories by 500 a day.)

A. Your weight in pounds: ______

B. Multiply A by 12 to get your basic calorie needs: ______

C. Multiply B by 1.6 to estimate your resting metabolic rate (calorie burn without factoring in exercise): ______

D. Strength training: Multiply the number of minutes you lift weights per week by 5: ______

E. Aerobic training: Multiply the number of minutes per week that you run, cycle, and play sports by 8: ______

F. Add D and E, and divide by 7: ______

G. Add C and F to get your daily calorie needs: ______

H. Add 500 to G: ______. *This is your estimated daily calorie needs to gain 1 pound a week.*

Work Big Not Small

Yes, biceps curls are fun, but if you want to put on muscle, you have to do more to challenge your body. And one key to doing that, says Samuel, is working through so-called "multi-joint" movements. "Yes, isolation training has value," says Samuel, "but it can't be the backbone of your training."Instead, you want to do exercises that challenge multiple joints and muscles at once. Take, for example, a dumbbell row. Every row rep challenges biceps, lats, and abs. Using multiple muscle groups allows you to lift more weight, says Samuel, a key stimulator of growth (more on that later). And it pushes you to use muscles together, just as you do in real life. "Multi-joint moves are key in your workouts," he says.

Make sure moves like squats, deadlifts, pullups, and bench presses are in your workout to take advantage of that. All will stimulate multiple muscle groups at the same time, and in order to grow, you want to do that.

Train Heavy

If you want to build muscle and strength, you have to train heavy, says Curtis Shannon C.S.C.S "Training heavy, safely and efficiently, has many benefits," says Shannon. "Heavy training challenges the muscles not only concentrically but eccentrically. If dont right, the stimulus of heavy weight going down with control and going back up will cause greater muscle tear and rebuild."

That means not every set you do should have you pumping out 10-15 reps. Yes, high-rep sets can have value, but for multi-joint moves like squats and bench presses, and deadlifts, don't be afraid to do sets of, say, 5 reps. That'll allow you to use more weight, building more pure strength, says Samuel. And as you progress, that new strength will allow you to lift heavier weights for more reps.

One way you can approach this in your training: Lead off every workout with an exercise that lets you train low-rep. Do 4 sets of 3-5 reps on your first exercise, then do 3 sets of 10-12 reps for every move after that. "It's the best of both worlds," says Samuel, "letting you build pure strength early, then pile up reps later."

Do Not Always Go Hard

Your body should move every day, but that doesn't mean your workouts should take you to fatigue and exhaustion. "If you train your hardest every day, your body doesn't get a chance to grow," says Samuel. "Pick your spots to attack." Aim to finish every workout feeling good, not dead. Limit your weight room workouts to 12-16 total sets of work, and never go beyond that.

This doesn't mean you can't take on a brutal workout every so often. But limit workouts that take your body to its breaking point to three times a week, never on back-to-back days. "You need recovery to grow," says Samuel. "Constantly training to the point of exhaustion will be counterproductive to the recovery you need for muscle growth."

Down The Carbs After Workout

Research shows that you'll rebuild muscle faster on your rest days if you feed your body carbohydrates.

"Post-workout meals with carbs increase your insulin levels," which, in turn, slows the rate of protein breakdown, says Kalman. Have a banana, a sports drink, a peanut-butter sandwich.

Challenge Yourself With Progessive Overload

As we mentioned earlier, one major key to muscle-building is pushing your muscles to handle progressively greater challenges. In general, most gym-goers think that means you must lift heavier in every single workout. That's simply not the case, says Samuel. "There comes a point where it becomes harder to just put more weight on the bar," he says. "If that wasn't the case, everyone would be benching 300 pounds."Don't simply aim to add weight on every set of every exercise, says Samuel. But do work to improve in some way on every set of an exercise. "Even if you're not going up in weight, you can push yourself in different ways," he says. "You might do 10 reps of *deadlifts this set. On the next set, instead of adding weight, do the same 10 reps, but do them with even sharper form."*

Sometimes, staying with the same weight for all four sets on a day can provide plenty of challenge, says Samuel, especially when you're improving your execution every set. There are other forms of progressive overload too. You can decrease the rest time between sets, going from, say, 120 seconds to 90 seconds, or you can up the reps, or you can even do more sets.

"Aim to improve every workout," says Samuel, "but know that that improvement won't always look the same. I may deadlift 315 pounds today 4 times and not be able to add weight. But if I can squeeze out a 5th rep, or even do my 4 reps with more control than I did last week, I'm on the right track."

Maximize Time Under Tension

One sometimes-forgotten way to progressively overload your muscles is to leave them under more of something called "time under tension". When you're muscles are working, whether they're under a bench press bar, or whether your biceps is working to curl a dumbbell upwards, they're under "tension" from the weight. You can feel this too: If you stand holding dumbbells at your sides, your biceps aren't under tension. The moment you begin to curl them upwards, you'll feel them flex against the "tension" of the dumbbells.Experienced lifters often use this tension to their advantage. Instead of just lifting and lowering a weight (on say, that biceps curl), they lift with a specific tempo. They might curl up as fast as they can, for example, and then lower the weight for 3 focused seconds with good form on every rep.

Doing this leaves your muscles under tension for longer than a typical set, in which you might lift and lower the weight without any specific timing. And that extra time under tension during a set can help spark muscle growth.

Note that you can do this on almost any strength exercise. It doesn't work for explosive exercises, like kettlebell swings, snatches, and cleans. But squats, deadlifts, curls, pullups and pushups (and many other moves) can be tweaked to add more time-under-tension, pushing your muscles farther on every rep.

Sleep At Least 6 Hours

We all know how much sleep is important not only in bodybuilding but also in every day to day work. If you do not take your sleep seriously then it can affect you in everything . you can not even do your daily work . Sleep plays a major role in your muscle building . Your body recovers during sleep, so no sleep means no muscle building .Sleep is often the forgotten variable in the journey to muscle. You spend plenty of time training, but what you often don't realize is this: When you're asleep, your muscles are recovering and your body is growing. It's also during this period that muscle-growing hormones are secreted.

You know by now that, ideally, you want to get 8 to 10 hours of sleep. That, of course, doesn't always happen, but you want to do what you can to maximize the quality of the hours you do get, if you can't hit 8 hours.

So think about your sleep setup if you're serious about muscle. Try to go to bed at the same time every day and try to rise at the same time every day. And sleep in a fully dark, fully quiet cool room. All these little things optimize sleep quality and that can have an underrated effect on your ability to build muscle.

ANOTHER BONUS TIP TO GIVE A BOOST IN YOUR MUSCLE BUILDING JOURNEY [Try At Your Own Risk]

Another thing which you can use to boost up your muscle building journey is ANABOLIC STEROIDS[AAS] and PED's [Performance Enhancing Drugs]

You oftenly see huge bodybuilders on TV and mobiles . They have such a huge physique which is not possible naturally that means you cannot grow this physique by following the above mentioned tips. You have to use these drugs .

WHAT ARE ANABOLIC STEROIDS

Ever wondered how those bulky weight lifters got so big? While some may have gotten their muscles through a strict regimen of weight-lifting and diet, others may have gotten that way through the illegal use of steroids.

Steroids are synthetic substances similar to the male sex hormone testosterone. They do have legitimate medical uses. Sometimes doctors prescribe anabolic steroids to help people with certain kinds of anemia and men who don't produce enough testosterone on their own. Doctors also prescribe a different kind of steroid, called corticosteroids, to reduce swelling. Corticosteroids are not anabolic steroids and do not have the same harmful effects.

But doctors never prescribe anabolic steroids to young, healthy people to help them build muscles. Without a prescription from a doctor, steroids are illegal.

There are many different kinds of steroids. Here's a list of some of the most common anabolic steroids taken today: anadrol, oxandrin, dianabol, winstrol, deca-durabolin, and equipoise.

USES

Some steroid users pop pills. Others use hypodermic needles to inject steroids directly into muscles. When users take more and more of a drug over and over again, they are called "abusers." Abusers have been known to take doses 10 to 100 times higher than the amount prescribed for medical reasons by a doctor.

Many steroid users take two or more kinds of steroids at once. Called stacking, this way of taking steroids is supposed to get users bigger faster. Some abusers pyramid their doses in 6-12-week cycles. At the beginning of the cycle, the steroid user starts with low doses and slowly increases to higher doses. In the second half of the cycle, they gradually decrease the amount of steroids. Neither of these methods has been proven to work.

SIDE EFFECTS

Steroids can make pimples pop up and hair fall out. They can make guys grow breasts and girls grow beards. Steroids can cause livers to grow tumors and hearts to clog up. They can even send users on violent, angry rampages. In other words, steroids throw a body way out of whack. Steroids do make users bulk up, but the health risks are high. It's true, on steroids biceps bulge; abs ripple; and quads balloon. But that's just on the outside. Steroid users may be very pleased when they flex in the mirror, but they may create problems on the inside. These problems may hurt them the rest of their lives. As a matter of fact steroid use can shorten their lives.

STEROIDS CAN CAUSE HORMONAL IMBALANCE

For teens, hormone balance is important. Hormones are involved in the development of a girl's feminine traits and a boy's masculine traits. When someone abuses steroids, gender mix-ups happen.

Using steroids, guys can experience shrunken testicles and reduced sperm count. They can also end up with breasts, a condition called gynecomastia.